The Invisible Ladder

The Invisible Ladder

Poems by

Michael Miller

© 2026 Michael Miller. All rights reserved.
This material may not be reproduced in any form, published,
reprinted, recorded, performed, broadcast,
rewritten or redistributed without
the explicit permission of Michael Miller.
All such actions are strictly prohibited by law.

Cover design by Shay Culligan
Cover image by Mick Haupt on Unsplash
Author photo by Harlon Miller

ISBN: 978-1-63980-845-8
Library of Congress Control Number: 2025950963

Kelsay Books
502 South 1040 East, A-119
American Fork, Utah 84003
Kelsaybooks.com

*For my grandchildren
Roscoe and Ruby*

Acknowledgments

Some of these poems, in slightly different versions, have appeared in the following journals:

Amethyst Review: New Writing Engaging with the Sacred

Chiron Review

Commonweal

Illuminations

Mudfish

The Orchards Poetry Journal

Poetry East

Quiet Diamonds 2024

Raritan

Salt

Tipton Poetry Journal

Weaving Shade: Contemporary Dream Poetry, An International Anthology (Lamar University Press, 2025)

Contents

I.

Solace	17
Questions	18
Calling at Night	19
The Birch in Winter	20
Skunk Cabbage	21
The Fall	22

II.

Together	29
Life Cycle	30
Swimming Laps	31
Emerging	32
Fidelity	33
Numinous	34

III.

Kaleidoscope	39
Finding Him	40
Stigma	41
Pearl S. Herman	42
The Ring	43
In the Blue Solarium	44
Miss Sweeney	45

IV.

Beginning Again	49
Waiting	50
Each Morning	51
Given Love	52
Paine's Creek Beach	53
Trust	54
Finality	55
Bricks and Mortar	56

V.

Pastel Foxes	59
Dreaming in Spring	60
Nocturne	61
Walking Slowly	62
Woman in Sunlight	63
Deep in the Woods	64
Mary Dempsey	65

VI.

Okinawa, 1959	69
On Leave in Kyoto	70
The Landing	71
Sumiko	72
War	73
The Return	74

Shrapnel	75
His Rifle	76
The Lieutenant	77

VII.

Knitting	81
Seeing the Crow	82
Talons	83
Choosing the Time	84
New Life	85
An Unexpected Peace	86
Quest	87

Glory be to God for dappled things—
*   For skies of couple—colour as a brinded cow;*
*   For rose-moles all in stipple upon trout that swim;*
Fresh-firecoal chestnut-falls; finches' wings;
*   Landscape plotted and pieced-fold, fallow, and plough;*
*   And all trades, their gear and tackle and trim.*

—Gerard Manley Hopkins

I.

Solace

He felt the need to separate
Himself from others
In a world not of his making.

His morning walk
Became the doorway
Into a house of light.

Nothing drew him more than
The cardinal's high-pitched call
From the pine top.

He practiced whistling
Until the cardinal
Returned his call.

Questions

Never forgotten
Was that Christmas morning
When he asked,
"Who was Jesus?"
And looking up from
Her newspaper, his mother saw
The curiosity in his eyes.

"He was a good man
Who helped people."
Satisfaction, silence,
A bond between them.
But he felt other questions
Brooding inside him,
Questions not for his mother.

Calling at Night

When he phones his daughter
In San Diego
Or his oldest friend
In Philadelphia
His first words
Will be exuberant
To avoid sounding vulnerable,
To conceal the fear
That he will close his eyes
For the last time.
Instantly their voices
Soothe his spirit
As it becomes a blue rose
He will name Tenderness
For the affection
He will offer endlessly.
He has never once
Picked a rose
From his garden,
Wanting each one
To unfold a life
Into light.

The Birch in Winter

As he stands before the birch
In the breathless air of winter,
The peeling scrolls of bark
Offer messages
About stillness, survival.
He moves closer and embraces
The trunk, his arms
A perfect fit as if he were
A welcomed friend.
Would this tree betray him?
Friends, those brothers
Of betrayal, have split his heart
Into unequal halves.
He will hold on to the birch,
Ready for the storm, the wind,
The thorns of ice.

Skunk Cabbage

In late April, off the trail
Through the woods, past the ferns
Swaying, a confusion
Of skunk cabbage thrives,
The new leaves curled into cones
Waiting to open, the large ones
Long and wavering.
He remembers the skunk
Living under the shed,
The small mound of cabbage
His mother served with corned beef,
But skunk cabbage was not like that.
He walked among it,
Opened his hands wide
And pretended to lift it
Into his arms, becoming green,
A giant cabbage towering over
Hundreds of others,
Leaving his days, his nights,
His dread growing
In dark corners.
How natural it would feel
To grow old in the woods!
His roots spreading through earth,
His leaves wilting in light,
His dying joined by the others.

The Fall

    I.   At Baystate

Sirened to the trauma unit
At Baystate
After my face-first fall
On the sidewalk
During an October afternoon,
The large clock in the room
With sealed windows
Devouring the past
Had no interest
In an old man
Nor in the scans,
The blue islands
From testing blood
Or my face with
Cuts and bruises
And a rosebud's red eye.
For five days
An explanation was sought,
My body a monitored machine—
Nothing was conclusive.
I was alive
In the peak of autumn
And waiting
For the spring.

II. Three Words

With haphazard white hair
The very old man
Opened his watery blue eyes
And said, "Dying is easy,"
Then leaned back in bed.
Why had the nurse left
The curtain opened between us?
Leaning forward again
He repeated, "Dying is easy."
And I wanted to draw the curtain
But asked instead,
"Can I get you anything?"
And his silence
Walked into my heart
To find its final place.

III. The Nurse

Trying to ignore
The levels of pain
As the healing
At home continues
In my eighty-fourth year,
I recall Cynthia's
Kindly touch
As she lifted me
In that hospital bed
To adjust the pillows—
Her caring was a balm
For my broken ribs.
I felt as if I had known
Cynthia long ago,
As if she had said
My name with her eyes.

IV.   Close

Time carries us forward,
Memory draws us backward.
I still remember
The directness of her stare
As she leaned
Close to my face
And said, "God bless you,"
After the doctor
Closed her father's eyes,
Then added,
"You were kind to him."

II.

Together

In their living room,
Near the roses in a vase
Beginning to wilt,
The grandfather clock
Chimed on the hour.
How old they were,
How young they felt
Each time they embraced,
Their wrinkles
Wedding them together.

On the pale blue wall
Facing their bed
A Chinese print
Of a colt bending over
To nibble the grass.
Looking at it before sleep
He feels like the colt,
She, the grass.

With their arms
Around each other
They drift toward sleep.
How wondrous it would be
To dream her dreams,
To offer her his own.

Life Cycle

After their daughter
Calls from Sarasota
A sun brightens within them.
Their grandchildren remind them
Of the continuity that unfolds
Like the perennials
In their garden,
Her favorite
The yellow-hearted
Crimson daylilies,
His, the purple irises.

Swimming Laps

With no one else in the pool
They swim laps together,
Their arms moving in unison
As they cut smoothly into water.

She was the natural,
He worked to keep up.
Time was at a standstill,
Old age forgotten.

Emerging

Mid-February
And the robins returned
To the bare branches
Of the sycamore.
She waited for the snowdrops
To appear like pearls;
He, for the tips
Of crocuses to push
Through the earth—
Soon they would emerge
From the cold,
From their cocoons.

Fidelity

Lying together
With nakedness
An unforgotten friend
Their breathing
Became a harmony.
Through the window
A welcoming breeze
Blew the lace curtain.
Words were unnecessary,
Fidelity was the language
Of their love.

Numinous

With trowel and hoe
They tended their garden.
Old age brought a harmony
That drew him back
To that afternoon decades ago
When they made love
The first time
In their wedding of silence.
That day harmony
Was all that mattered.

She has never stopped
Wearing the thin gold cross
He felt when his body
Pressed upon hers
In sunlight
Falling through the window
To warm his back
Like a shawl.
Neither of them mentioned divinity
But felt its presence.

When they separated
And lay on their backs
He thought that God
Was in their bodies
And their bodies
Were their souls.

During her six-hour surgery
He tried to read
In the lounge,
Then walked the halls,
Went out to the garden
And with all the faith
Of his twenty-two yeas
Prayed before the blossoms.
When the doctor approached
In his loose-fitting gown
He thought of a blue angel.
"She's fine," he said with a smile,
"There was no bleeding."
And he tried to speak
But gratitude
Choked his words.

III.

Kaleidoscope

In a kaleidoscope of images
Past merges with present
In a realm more space than time.
Here my grandmother
Plucks the white hairs
Above her lip with a tweezer,
My mother hurries
Off to work,
My son and grandchildren
Decorate a Christmas tree
And I am lifted
Into a world of surprise
Beyond those judgments
That become burdens
Weighing me down.
I turn the kaleidoscope
Not knowing what
Will next appear.

Finding Him

I first heard about God
From my peasant grandmother
Who wore a housedress
Dappled with pink roses
And played solitaire
At the kitchen table.
Each time she turned over
A king she mumbled,
"Thank you, God."
When I asked her
About God she told me
To find Him for myself.
"Where should I look?"
"Everywhere," she replied,
And I looked into her
Blue eyes and didn't see Him.
He wasn't in the plants
By the window
Or the cookie jar.
I would keep looking.

Stigma

What did I know about
The invisible D for divorce
In 1945, the stigma?
Sunday was not a family day,
My mother never took me
To the park, the zoo,
The Museum of Natural History
When it rained.
All my mother did on Sundays
Was read the thick paper.
I read the funnies
On the floor, my favorite,
Handsome Prince Valiant.
Years later she said,
"I left your father,
He said he would kill you."

Pearl S. Herman

From a safe distance
I followed her,
The nearest person
To beauty I knew,
My sixth-grade teacher
Pearl S. Herman who lived
Three blocks from school.
I looked down her tan suit
To long shapely legs
In stockings with
A singular seam.
I yearned to
Stroke those legs,
My eleventh year
Passion aroused.

The Ring

Dinner was liver
With onions on top
And my silence.
What could I say to this man
I would call Jack?
Soon I wished
He was my father,
This reticent man
My mother loved,
This Marine who fought
On Guadalcanal,
Who never spoke of his
Purple Heart, his Bronze Star.
His Catholic hand
Taught me right from wrong.
I refused to wince
When the back of it
Struck my cheek.
I felt his tough love
Strengthen my spirit.
Today I wear his ring.
I kiss the blue sapphire
That left its mark.

In the Blue Solarium

His large hazel eyes
Drew my attention
Before his thick tongue
Struggled as he began to speak
On the first day
Of seventh grade,
His red hair parted on the side,
The wave a crest of flame.

Gerard became my friend,
No one called him retard
In my presence,
His strong hand gripped mine
With a need for connection,
His love a different flower
Unfolding.

Seventy-one years have passed
And I visit Gerard every Saturday
Assured he will be waiting
In the blue solarium
At two o'clock.
He will take me
To the community garden,
Lead me to every flower
And say its name,
His faded red hair
Streaked with gray.

Miss Sweeney

A ruddy face, a wealth of curly
Gray hair, her eyes a turquoise ocean
Advancing into me—"Learn what adaptable
Means," she said, and I recognized
Miss Sweeney, principal,
Instructing me in a dream.

Forgotten through my calendar of years
She appeared, brandishing
Her word of the month:
Adaptable, written in bold green
Letters on posters in the hall.

Dear Miss Sweeney, you were telling me
To adapt to loss, to blindness,
The shadows looming over my old age.
I woke from my dream,
Adaptable, to begin the day.

IV.

Beginning Again

Like patient strangers
Our bodies waited
To be rediscovered
In our forty-second spring,
Then hands and lips touched
When we met by chance,
Two people alone
After failures in love
Who lost themselves
In choices wrong enough
To blame.
Moving slowly,
Still wary of mistakes,
We grew closer
Giving trust a place.

Waiting

As we undressed in lamplight
I waited for you
To lead my body
To your places of passion
Before we settled in bed.
There I patiently lay
As you began to write on a page
In your book of lust.
I read your cursive slowly
As if it were meant for me,
Pausing at every comma, every period.
There was never a rush to finish.

Each Morning

The tall windows
Of the Dickinson home
Face the Pelham Hills
Where the eastern light
Gives way to a crimson wash
Undisturbed by a wide-winged
Great blue heron crossing
That pathway of sky
Emily could see
From the second floor.
On a wooden bench
Beside her garden
I watch the sunrise
Each morning
Which brings me
A solitary delight.
I feel sad for not
Asking you to join me—
It's only a ten-minute walk—
But I accept the man I am
As you have accepted him,
The tenderness and tumult
Still willing to bind us.
Love asks for little,
And accepts what we give
Like Emily baking her
Father's favorite bread
Each morning, awaiting
His horse-drawn carriage
As the sun declines.

Given Love

Beautiful tree, the boys
In high school called you.
Far from that time I agree.
Now after decades
Words cannot describe
My feelings when I look
Into your leaves that
Hold a night containing
Time remembered,
Time adding to the dimensions
Of our given love.
Differences and changes
Have altered little.
Beyond our comprehension,
What I call God
And you call the mystery
Has blessed us as we
Look into the trees
In our old age.

Paine's Creek Beach

A keeper of the past
I return to Paine's Creek Beach
After reaching deep
Into my need
For unforgotten images:
Tall sea grass
Stood with yellow blades
Accepting the incoming tide
That broke like ruffled lace
To wash away the prints
Of scrabbling crabs
Hiding among barnacled rocks.
Our deeper footprints
Lingered longer
Before they disappeared
Into the rippled sand
Where sea-polished
Bits of glass
Shone like emeralds.
How content we were
In that place
Where we lived with
The sea and the sky
And the long-legged sandpiper
That stopped in its tracks
To stare at us
As we stared back,
Two beings driven
By the same curiosity
Born each new day.

Trust

In your memory
My innocence
Approaches your own
As we begin to climb up
The invisible ladder
Forty-two years ago
Not knowing what to expect.

I trusted my feelings,
Sensing in them
The infinite
Merging with yours
As we drew into
This place of understanding,
Of empathy.

Finality

I enter our room
And see you in the lamplight,
The beautiful more apparent
In your richness of years.

We adapt, we move carefully
Through our lives with their
Collection of diminishments.
Nothing has made me happier
Than our house of expanding love,
Its unknown rooms
A discovery each day.

Should your last breath
Be drawn before mine
I will kiss the death
On your lips and hope
It will soon be mine.

In the room of imagination
We are lying in adjacent beds
Connected to a mutual heart monitor,
A gentle melody
Plays from a speaker
Lifting us through death
Into a place where souls join.
The monitor stops,
The silence reigns,
We are becoming
The space between stars.

Bricks and Mortar

The hollowness inside me
Was different from the hunger,
My need to seek and find
Love in a youth lacking
Discipline but not dimension.
The architecture of passion
Has never left me,
I keep the plans
In a zippered pocket,
A stooped man who raises
His arms like wings
When he tilts
And momentarily loses
His balance
But not his enriching love
For a woman with goodness
Rooted in her heart.
No matter the frustrations
And diminishments
Of growing old
We go on, still building
With bricks and mortar
What unfinished love requires.

V.

Pastel Foxes

"Not tonight," he says to death,
"Tomorrow my daughter and granddaughter
Will come." He has always loved women;
Making gingerbread cookies with his mother,
Rolling the dough, waiting eagerly
For her next direction.
What a melodious voice she had
Teaching him to read
As he leaned against her on the couch.
When she went to the hairdresser
He wrapped her fox piece
Around his shoulders,
Stroking the small pointed head.
In his eighty-first year
H draws foxes, pastel foxes
He hopes to bring
To his mother in a dream.

Dreaming in Spring

He dreams of walking
Along Heatherstone Road
Toward their house
After leaving tropical
New Orleans decades ago—
Birches and sugar maples
Replaced swamp magnolias,
His young southern wife
Vibrantly alive.

Together, they planted, weeded,
Made their first garden
With daffodils
Like trumpets.
If only he could awaken
And be in that garden.
In his eighty-fifth spring
His dream renews the closeness
That was lost too long ago.

Nocturne

Waiting for the invisible hands
Of sleep to lift him from
The loneliness of another day
He sits in his fraying chair
With his eyes opened
Like a blind man
Who has seen so much pain
And wept for so long
That his pupils
Have been washed away.
Without the presence of mind
He turns toward the dark window
Almost as dark
As the darkness within him—
The light has vanished
From his life.
But he remembers
How they fell asleep
In each other's arms,
A nocturne by Chopin
Playing softly at midnight.
Years have passed
Since that night a week
Before her death
When the nocturne
Became a lullaby
Soothing her remaining fear.
There must be a music
That is still in his soul,
A music that is playing,
Waiting for him.

Walking Slowly

When her knees feel
Like egg shells cracking
She reaches for her cane
And begins her morning walk,
Looking up at the arrowhead
Of geese, their undersides
Brightened by the sunrise,
Looking down at the line of ants
Like a shoelace
Across the sidewalk.
Walking slowly allows her
To see more, miss less
And focus closely.
Too much of her life
Ha been hurried.
Slowing down implies
A deeper vision,
A more observant eye,
A smile for the bluebird
In a crowd of leaves.

Woman in Sunlight

In Sweetser Park the woman said
Drink all you want to the wrens
Arriving at the fountain
In early morning sunlight,
Her three shopping bags
Overflowing with belongings
On the wooden bench
With cigarette butts
By her bare feet.
This is the New England town
Where stoic faces pass her by,
This is where he stops to place
A muffin from the bakery
On the bench beside her,
This is the tangled-haired woman
With a wilderness,
A childhood in her eyes.

Deep in the Woods

On that summer day
Heavy with heat
As he spread
His mother's ashes
On the brown needles
In a cathedral of pine
And covered them
With a flat rock
He felt a closeness to her
Missing from his life.
"We've never been close,"
She once said,
And he wanted to reply,
"Whose fault is that?"
Words going unsaid
Finally wrote their cursive
Across his heart.

Mary Dempsey

Above the shrouded hills
An orange sun
Brought vivid light
To her old age.
She faced it on the sidewalk
Near her gray-shingled house
As she gripped the handles
Of her trusted walker,
A woman in love
With each new day
Who never thought
About death.
Today was for her,
The warm breeze
Whispered good morning
As she replied with
Her wrinkled smile
That contained her decades,
Then remembered
The new book shelf
Waiting at the library.

VI.

Okinawa, 1959

He hiked the unruly jungle:
Vines wrapped around trees,
Snakes slipped between
Bayonets of grass,
The Suicide Cliffs
A stark reminder
Of World War Two.
In a recreation retreat,
On a deserted beach,
He escaped the training
To kill, spending
His days swimming,
His nights gazing
At a path of moonlight
Dividing the sea.
He loved, he hated
The Marine Corps.

On Leave in Kyoto

In the Japanese scholar's garden
Where a black swan
Glided across a pond

He imagined its closed wings
Were the pages of darkness
Containing a history of ruins.

What should he name this swan?
Hiroshima, a voice said,
Name it Hiroshima.

The Landing

Wading through the water
Toward the black sand
Of Iwo Jima
With his rifle held high
He knew it was God
That kept him alive
After the Marine four yards away
Was blown into pieces
That slashed his face
With blood he felt was his own.
This was the only time
He spoke to me of the war,
Of the landing,
Not the battle.

Sumiko

At a corner table
In the shaded light
Of the Jade Restaurant
Sumiko cut her hamburger,
Wrapped half of it
With a napkin to bring
To her mother
As his eighteen-year-old heart
Broke into quiet pieces.
This bar girl
With her captivating air,
With a goodness
Nothing could change,
Drew him away from
The Marines.
He never wanted
To leave her.

War

Considering himself lucky
To be alive he will never
Tell a war story,
That inaccurate word
Rousing an old anger inside him.
Why pass one horror
Or a hundred to a son,
A friend, a boon companion
In a barroom for a night?
Boyhood war games
Are best left in boyhood,
War movies a contrivance
Pretending to be real.
Certain novels approach
The stark reality of battle,
An approach far from true.
Stories are meant for campfires
And toasting marshmallows,
War has no place except
For those who fought in one.
War spelled backwards is raw.

The Return

Naked beside his wife
On his first night home
He closed his eyes.
The war was over
But would never be over.
As lightly as a fern
Her hand moved over his body
Careful to avoid
The scars of battle.
He was safe.
He opened his eyes.
"Why was I spared?"

Shrapnel

He has learned to almost love
The scar on his chest
Where the hair will never grow.
Each night he faithfully
Moves his fingers across it
As he travels toward sleep.
He imagines the shrapnel
Like a butterfly flying out
Of the operating room
At Walter Reed
And back to Afghanistan
Where he returns in nightmares
As a hundred steel butterflies
Float above his body
Wounded in the sand
Of Kandahar.

His Rifle

Only in his dream does he forget
That his rifle was used for killing.
Only in his dream does he dismantle it
With the same care that his hands
Once bestowed upon his dying mother
In her house in Wilmington, North Carolina,
Where he searched for pieces of
Broken glass smoothed by the sea,
His polished treasure on the rippled sand
At low tide. If only he were that boy
In his dream and not an ex-Marine
Dismantling his rifle and loving the parts,
The trigger, the bolt, that he cleans
To perfection; he does not assemble them
Into the weapon he used to kill
The Taliban who kept on coming,
Who will always be coming

The Lieutenant

He drinks in his chair
As midnight sinks
Into the new day.
He lowers his head
As his face rests
Between his scarred hands—
The scars from reaching
Into the flaming Humvee
To pull out Garcia
Seem to belong
To another man.
He closes his eyes,
Sees Wilson bleeding out
From shrapnel
Jutting from his neck
Pumping out blood
He cannot stop—
Why isn't there a corpsman?
He opens his eyes
And swallows the last
Of the bourbon.
"Who lives, who dies?" he asks,
A questioning lieutenant
Accustomed to orders
Without explanations.
Opening a new bottle
He thinks of primeval man

Killing with clubs.
He knows his war
Will never end.

His Silver Star
Belongs to a different man.
The lieutenant bars
Once on his shoulders
Now weigh him down.

VII.

Knitting

The knitting needles
Fit perfectly between her fingers
As they moved with
A rhythm from within
Until gray and white wool
Like a wolf's winter coat
Became a quilt,
A connection
For continuous love
Between husband and wife
After she lost him in autumn.
When the quilt was done
In the first week of December
She spread it on
His side of the bed,
Curling up with it
During the night,
Imagining it was his body,
Warm, protective.

Seeing the Crow

On a sun starved morning
She makes deep tracks
In unmarked snow
Leading to the bare magnolia.
She will not disturb the crow
Perched in silence
On the top branch.
Inhaling the fragrance
Of pink-edged white blossoms
In spring was as easy
As seeing the crow as crow
In the dead end of December.
The crow looks down at her,
The connection made.

Talons

He saw the white head,
The folded brown wings
As this bullet of a bird
Plummeted toward its victim,
Hooked talons striking,
Seizing, clutching,
Pressing the limp rabbit
Against the field
As the stabbing beak
Began its diligent work
Extracting pieces of life.
The eagle continued to eat
With enviable hunger,
Its yellow eyes
Containing centuries.
Finished, it lifted off
The field, disappeared
Beyond the trees.
He hoped his death
Would be as sudden,
As swift.

Choosing the Time

She chose her time
And comfortable place
To stop eating
In her ninety-second spring
When that crab
Made itself known again
In her uncomplaining body.
Three friends attended her
With indispensable love,
Wiping her brow
With a cool cloth,
Placing a straw
Between her lips.
Each night they read
Her favorite poems,
Held up photographs
Of her lush garden
As she eased toward
That ultimate sleep
With the gratitude
That replaced regrets.

New Life

After my granddaughter
Entered our living room
For the first time
Her three-year-old directness
Approached my worn chair
As she leaned close to my face
And said, "You have blue eyes."
This was our introduction,
The beginning of a new life
In my old age
Without a single obstacle.

An Unexpected Peace

At dusk he lay beside
Her gravestone and felt
An unexpected peace,
His lips unwhispering
As the grass
Beneath his body.
No wind cut a path
Through the air,
His undelivered thoughts
Had been left
In an envelope
Waiting to be mailed.
He knew the moon
Would shortly rise
Indifferent to his
Slow walk home.
There he would sit
In her chair,
Put on her glasses
And see through her eyes.

Quest

He began his quest for faith
As a boy kneeling
Before his bed looking for God
Between his hands.
Now a white-haired man
He finds his continuing monologue
Filled with questions unanswered.
Having aged into patience
He sees God
In the glistening spider web
Stretching across the hedge
In sunlight after the rain.
What he has learned
Through doubt and belief
Is that God is in his
Morning walks at sunrise
As he looks at
A black-masked cedar waxwing
On a maple branch
Or listens to the song
Of a thrush unseen.

About the Author

Michael Miller's first book, *The Joyful Dark,* was the Editor's Choice winner of The McGovern Prize at Ashland Poetry Press. His third book, *Darkening the Grass,* was a "Must Read" selection of The Massachusetts Book Award (2013). His poem "The Different War" was the 2014 First Prize Winner of the W.B. Years Society Poetry Award and was anthologized in *Yeats 150* (Lilliput Press, Dublin). His poems have appeared in *The Kenyon Review, the Sewanee Review, The New Republic, The American Scholar, Ontario Review, The Southern Review, Commonweal, Raritan, The Michigan Quarterly Review,* and other journals and anthologies. Born in 1940, Michael Miller served four years in the Marine Corps. He lives in Amherst, Massachusetts.

www.ingramcontent.com/pod-product-compliance
Lightning Source LLC
Chambersburg PA
CBHW031202160426
43193CB00008B/478